Serbian Cooking
POPULAR RECIPES FROM THE BALKAN REGION

Danijela Kracun and Charles McFadden

4880 Lower Valley Road • Atglen, PA 19310

Author's Note

Although most of the recipes in this book are vegetarian, feel free to add any meat of your choice to the recipes!

I hope you find the recipes in this book simple and delicious. For the most part they are healthy—except for some of the decadent desserts!

Other Schiffer Books by the Authors:

Contemporary Painters
ISBN: 978-0-7643-4108-3

Contemporary Sculptors: 84 International Artists
ISBN: 978-0-7643-4103-8

Creative Glass
ISBN: 978-0-7643-3505-1

Spiritual Gardens: A Guide to Meditating in Nature
ISBN: 978-0-7643-3731-4

Copyright © 2015 by Danijela Kracun and Charles McFadden
Library of Congress Control Number: 2014950508

All rights reserved. No part of this work may be reproduced or used in any form or by any means—graphic, electronic, or mechanical, including photocopying or information storage and retrieval systems—without written permission from the publisher.

The scanning, uploading, and distribution of this book or any part thereof via the Internet or via any other means without the permission of the publisher is illegal and punishable by law. Please purchase only authorized editions and do not participate in or encourage the electronic piracy of copyrighted materials.
"Schiffer," "Schiffer Publishing, Ltd. & Design," and the "Design of pen and inkwell" are registered trademarks of Schiffer Publishing, Ltd.

Designed by John P. Cheek
Type set in Staccato/Gotham

ISBN: 978-0-7643-4760-3
Printed in China

Published by Schiffer Publishing, Ltd.
4880 Lower Valley Road
Atglen, PA 19310
Phone: (610) 593-1777; Fax: (610) 593-2002
E-mail: Info@schifferbooks.com

For our complete selection of fine books on this and related subjects, please visit our website at
www.schifferbooks.com.
You may also write for a free catalog.

This book may be purchased from the publisher. Please try your bookstore first.

We are always looking for people to write books on new and related subjects. If you have an idea for a book, please contact us at proposals@schifferbooks.com.

Schiffer Publishing's titles are available at special discounts for bulk purchases for sales promotions or premiums. Special editions, including personalized covers, corporate imprints, and excerpts can be created in large quantities for special needs. For more information, contact the publisher.

This book is dedicated to food lovers and eaters everywhere!

Also to my awesome children—Tim, Sam, and Paisley—and my nieces and nephews—Cameron, Kordy, Lucia, and Tristan.

Happy eating!

Acknowledgments

Thanks to my mom for cooking these fabulous meals and teaching me how to be a good cook—and for going against her nature and making all of the recipes vegetarian!

Thanks to my wonderful kids for inspiring the book and convincing me that "yellow" deserves to be in a cookbook. You guys make me smile every day and remind me that life is like a recipe, a little of this and a little of that all mixed together makes something delicious.

Thank you to Ivana Lalicki for providing some of the delicious recipes and pictures. Radovan and Wendy Jacovic for welcoming us to their Balkan Express Restaurant. Check out Ivana Laicki's blog at Ivana Lalicki, Dolce Fooda, www.dolcefooda.blogspot.com and www.soibiber.blogspot.com. Visit Radovan and Wendy's Balkan Express Restaurant in Philadelphia, Pennsylvania.

Contents

Introduction 6

APPETIZERS 7

    Bread (Hleb) 9
    Coffee (Kafa) 10
    French Toast (Kvasenice) 11
    Eggs and Onions (Luka I Jaja) 12
    Cheese Biscuits (Pogacice sa Sirom) 13
    Fried Potatoes (Pomfrit) 14
    Cold Cuts Platter (Srpska Zakuska) 15
    Plum Dumplings (Gomboce) 17
    Cornbread (Proja) 19
    Cabbage Salad 20
    Cauliflower 21
    Yellow (Zuto) 23

ENTREES 25

    Burek with Meat (Burek sa Mesom) 27
    Burek with Cheese (Burek sa Sirom) 29
    Christmas Bread (Cesnica) 31
    Cevapi 33
    Chicken Paprikash with Peas (Grasak) 35
    Lentil Soup 37
    Dill Sauce (Beli Sos) 38
    Djuvec 39
    Cheese Danish (Gibanica) 40
    Koh 41
    Kommisbrot 43
    Potato Salad (Krompir Salata) 45
    Chicken Paprikash 47
    Cauliflower Soup 48
    Rice and Onions (Luk I Pirinadz) 49

    Potato Pita (Pita sa Krompirom) 50
    Mushroom Filo Pie 51
    Cabbage with Sausage and Bacon 52
    Tomato Sauce 53
    Potato Casserole 55
    Baked Beans (Prebranac) 57
    Stuffed Peppers (Punjene Paprike) 59
    Ribs on Chef 61
    Sataras 63
    Sweet Cabbage with Beef and/or Pork ... 65
    Roasted Peppers with Cheese (Pecene Paprike) 67

DESSERTS 69

    Honey Wafers 71
    Baklava 73
    Cupavci 75
    Cherry Strudel 77
    Bombica 78
    Chocolate Balls 79
    Chestnut Cake 81
    Chocolate Rolls 83
    Chocolate Wafers 85
    Crème Puffs 87
    Crepes 89
    Peach Pie 91
    Poppy Seed Strudel 93
    Tulumbe 95
    Vanilla Wafers 97
    Walnut Strudel 99
    Vanilla Pastry 101

Measurement and Equivalency Charts 102
Conclusion 103
About the Authors 104

Introduction

Serbian Cooking

Now that I am almost forty years old and thinking back on my own cultural background, it amazes me how far from nature we have strayed in our daily cooking. While growing up in a small city in the country of Serbia, I ate fresh food grown by my parents and grandparents. I was not raised with a microwave, nor do I use one today in my own kitchen. I did, however, get to enjoy fresh food that was brought directly to the table from our own personal garden that my family tended to every day. How lucky was I? Nowadays, with the constant debate over GMO foods, I feel I lived in luxury. But most people back then would, I am sure, not view their life in that way. Everyday, my grandmother tended to the chickens and brought fresh eggs to the table. We had seasonal vegetables—which did not have their own name back in the day: I am talking about macrobiotic. I find it almost comical that we name a most natural way of eating as a reminder of what it is. Even so, cooking was simple, healthy, and delicious.

I had the privilege of growing up with parents and in a country that valued organic food and every household grew their own vegetables and raised their own livestock. The meats were fresh, the vegetables seasonal and all of the wonderful baked goods—well, I will let the pictures speak for themselves about that.

My family was never big on soda, and we still drink very little of it. I do wish I had the ability to grow my own food and livestock. Serbian families ate what they grew and had room to raise. If you had room on your land for a lot of vegetables, great, your family had variety; if not, oftentimes people shared their vegetables. The same thing was true for meats. If you had enough room for chickens, pigs, turkey, and whatever else you chose to eat, great! If not, you ate what you had room to raise. My family focused on chickens and pigs. I think my first real hamburger was in the U.S. when I was in high school.

I have grown up to be a vegetarian and my three kids mostly eat vegetarian-type dishes. But I do come from a heavy meat-eating background. My grandfather was a butcher and I loved watching him work. I terrorize my kids with stories from the old country and often miss the days of simple living and eating.

Most of the Serbian culture and cooking is intertwined with the local countries of Europe. At one point, Serbia was part of Austria-Hungary, so it is natural that many of the dishes will seem similar if not exactly the same to some of your own old-country dishes. If we look at the history of the region, you will find a very mixed group of people who, for the most part, live well together and get along—especially when food is involved; it somehow brings everyone together.

The serving sizes of the recipes and food may look a little small to you. A typical day in Serbia is normally not concentrated upon food. Food definitely brings the family together and is always offered to a guest; however, it is not about glutinous eating.

Many shops in Europe, as a whole, will close in the middle of the day and the workers will go home and enjoy lunch with their family. Lunch in Serbia is the biggest meal of the day. Breakfast is usually focused on a protein of a sort, with a light beverage, such as tea or milk. The afternoon snack may be a baked pastry, or an outing with friends for coffee and dessert. Dinner just happens to be the lightest meal of the day, typically involving on cold cuts, bread, and beverage.

As I mentioned, soda was rarely part of a meal…

I hope you enjoy the recipes in this book and, if you are ever in Europe, stop by and check out Serbia!

APPETIZERS

Cold Cuts Platter (Srpska Zakuska). *Photo by Tanja*

Bread. *Photo by Nelabooks, courtesy of Balkan Express Restaurant, Philadelphia, PA.*

Bread
(Hleb)

SERVES 4-6

Ingredients

1 cup milk
2 tablespoons butter
1½ cups warm water
2 packages active dry yeast
2 tablespoons sugar
1 tablespoon salt
6-7 cups of unbleached bread flour

Directions

Heat milk and butter in a small saucepan over medium heat. Remove from heat when the butter is melted. Set aside to cool.

Pour ½ cup warm water into a small bowl. Slowly pour yeast into bowl while stirring. The constant stirring while adding the yeast will prevent the dry yeast from clumping. Set the bowl of yeast water aside for about 5 minutes while you work on the next 2 steps.

In a large bowl, add sugar, salt, and 1 cup of warm water. Mix.

Check the small saucepan of milk and butter. If the contents are warm to the touch, pour the liquid into the large bowl and mix.

Pour the yeast water into the large bowl. It is important that the batter is warm, not boiling hot. Hot liquid, such as the milk you heated up, will kill the dry yeast and prevent the bread from rising.

Begin mixing in the unbleached bread flour, one cup at a time. By the fifth cup of flour, the dough will begin to get stiff and it will be difficult to mix it with a wooden spoon. Turn dough out onto a floured board and begin to knead the dough. Continue adding more flour and kneading the flour into the dough until the dough is smooth, not sticky.

Next, grease a large bowl with butter. Put the bread dough into the bowl and then turn the dough over so that the top of the dough is now buttered. Cover the bowl with a kitchen towel and let the dough rise at room temperature until double in size or about 1 hour.

Punch down dough. Turn it out onto a floured board and knead out all the bubbles for about 5 minutes. Divide the dough in half and form each half into a loaf by first rolling the dough into a rectangle, and then rolling the dough up like a jellyroll. Pinch seam closed. Pinch and tuck edges under the loaf.

Preheat oven to 375 degrees F. Butter two loaf pans. Spread a light layer of yellow cornmeal on the loaf pans, if desired. Set loaves in pans, cover with a kitchen towel, and allow to rise until double in size or for about a half hour.

Bake bread for about 45 minutes or until golden brown. Remove bread from oven and turn out loaves onto a rack or a clean kitchen towel. Allow to cool before cutting.

Coffee
(Kafa)

SERVES 4-6

Ingredients

2 cups water
2 teaspoons sugar
2 teaspoons finely ground coffee

Directions

Bring water and sugar to boil.
Add coffee.
Reduce to simmer and stir until froth begins to form.
Pour into cups and enjoy!

Coffee. Photo by Ivana Lalicki, Dolce Fooda.

French Toast
(Kvasenice)

SERVES 4-6

Ingredients

2 eggs
½ cup milk
Loaf of bread
2 tablespoons olive oil
Salt and pepper

Directions

Mix eggs with milk in a bowl, and soak bread slices in the mixture.

Heat two tablespoons of olive oil in medium-sized pan over low heat. Add the soaked bread once the pan is hot. Toast one side until golden. Flip and toast other side until golden. Salt and pepper to taste.

French Toast. Photo by Nelabooks.

Eggs and Onions
(Luka I Jaja)

SERVES 4-6

Ingredients

½ onion, chopped
1 red and/or green pepper, chopped
¼ cup olive oil
5-6 eggs, beaten
Salt and pepper to taste
Dill for garnish

Directions

In medium saucepan, sauté onion and pepper in oil over medium heat. Beat eggs and add to pan. Mix together until eggs are fluffy. Salt and pepper to taste.

Eggs and Onions. *Photo by Nelabooks.*

Cheese Biscuits
(Pogacice sa Sirom)

SERVES 4-6

Ingredients

1⅓ cups all-purpose flour
1 teaspoon baking powder
1 teaspoon fennel seeds, crushed
½ teaspoon sugar
¼ teaspoon salt
¼ teaspoon baking soda
6 tablespoons cold butter, cut up
2 ounces (½ cup) sharp provolone or cheddar cheese, shredded
1 ounce (about ⅓ cup) thinly sliced prosciutto or cooked ham, finely chopped
½ cup milk

Cheese Biscuits. *Photo by Ivana Lalicki, Dolce Fooda.*

Directions

Preheat oven to 425 degrees F. In a medium bowl stir together flour, baking powder, fennel seeds, sugar, salt, and baking soda. Using a pastry blender, cut in butter until flour mixture resembles coarse crumbs. Stir in cheese and prosciutto.

Make a well in center of flour mixture; add milk all at once. Using a fork, stir just until moistened. Turn dough out onto a lightly floured surface. Knead dough by folding and gently pressing 4 to 6 strokes or just until dough holds together. Lightly roll dough to 9- x 5-inch rectangle. Using a long knife or pizza cutter, cut dough lengthwise in half, then crosswise in fourths, making 8 rectangles.

Roll up rectangles and arrange dough pieces on ungreased baking sheet. Bake 12 to 14 minutes or until biscuits are golden brown; remove from baking sheet and serve warm. Makes 8 biscuits.

Fried Potatoes
(Pomfrit)

SERVES 4-6

Ingredients

4 potatoes, cut into slices
⅓ cup plus 2 tablespoons olive oil
Vegeta® seasoning

Directions

Cut potatoes like steak fries. Roll into about 2 tablespoons of olive oil. Add Vegeta® seasoning.

Heat remaining olive oil in medium-sized pan over medium heat. Make sure pan is hot. Add potatoes and continue to stir until golden brown.

Fried Potatoes. *Photo by Nelabooks.*

Cold Cuts Platter
(Srpska Zakuska)

Directions

Arrange various cold cuts and other foods, including the must-haves of olives, goat cheese, and lettuce.

Cold Cuts Platter (Srpska Zakuska). *Photo by Tanja.*

Plum Dumplings. Photo by Ivana Lalicki, Dolce Fooda.

Plum Dumplings
(Gomboce)

SERVES 4-6

Ingredients

5 medium potatoes, peeled, boiled, mashed, and cooled
2 large eggs
1 teaspoon salt
2½ cups all-purpose flour
18 damson or Italian prune plums, washed and pitted
4 tablespoons (½ stick) butter
1½ cups very fine bread crumbs
¼ cup cinnamon sugar

Plum Dumplings. *Photo by Ivana Lalicki, Dolce Fooda.*

Directions

In a large bowl, combine potatoes, eggs, and salt. When well combined, add flour and mix until a soft dough forms. Cover with plastic wrap and let rest 30 minutes.

Place a large pot of salted water on to boil. On a lightly floured surface, roll dough to ⅓ inch. Cut into 2-inch squares. Place a plum in the center of each square and fold in half, pressing out all air and sealing the edges. Moisten edges before crimping if necessary to seal. Carefully drop into boiling water. Repeat until all plums are in the water. Cook 30 minutes.

Meanwhile, melt butter in large skillet, add bread crumbs, and cook until brown. Using a slotted spoon, remove dumplings to a colander to drain. Place dumplings in skillet, coating with buttered crumbs. Transfer to a serving platter and sprinkle with cinnamon sugar.

Cornbread (Proja). Photo by Tanja.

Cornbread
(Proja)

SERVES 4-6

Ingredients

5 eggs
2½ cups (20 ounces) olive oil
¼ cup cream
About 2 cups corn flour
1 12-ounce bottle of mineral water
1¼ cups polenta
10½ ounces mozzarella cheese, grated
Salt to taste

Directions

Mix eggs, oil, and cream together. Add corn flour, mineral water, polenta, and cheese. Place in a greased 9-inch baking pan in oven and bake at 300 degrees F. for 30-45 minutes.

Cornbread (Proja). Photo by Tanja.

Cabbage Salad

SERVES 4-6

Ingredients

1 small cabbage, cut in two, then grated
Salt and pepper to taste
Olive oil and vinegar to taste (2 to 1 ratio)
Pinch of garlic, minced
Parsley, for garnish

Directions

Grate cabbage. In a bowl, whisk together salt, pepper, olive oil, and vinegar, then add a pinch of garlic. Mix in cabbage. Garnish servings with parsley, if desired.

Cabbage Salad

Cauliflower

SERVES 4-6

Ingredients

1 cauliflower head
2 eggs, beaten
1 cup olive oil
Salt and pepper to taste

Directions

Boil cauliflower head for 5 to 10 minutes. Cut into small pieces. Dip pieces in the egg wash.

Heat the oil in a large skillet over low heat. Place the cauliflower into the hot oil. Cook until golden brown.

Cauliflower. Photo by Nelabooks.

Yellow. *Photo by Nelabooks.*

Yellow
(Zuto)

SERVES 4-6

Ingredients

2 eggs
2 tablespoons flour
Vegeta® seasoning to taste
¼ cup olive oil

Directions

Mix first three ingredients together and then fry in a pan with olive oil.

If feeling frisky, you can add cheese, cauliflower that has been boiled and mashed, and prosciutto.

ENTREES

Ribs on Chef. *Photo by Tanja.*

Burek with Meat. *Photo by Nelabooks.*

Burek with Meat
(Burek sa Mesom)

SERVES 4-6

Ingredients

½ pound ground chuck
½ pound lean ground pork
(Eliminate the pork and use more beef and/or lamb, if desired)
½ pound lean ground lamb
1 large onion, finely chopped

1 garlic clove, finely chopped
1½ teaspoons salt
Pepper to taste
1 pound package thawed filo dough

¼ cup vegetable, sunflower, or pumpkin oil
4 large eggs, beaten
1½ cups soda water

Directions

In a large skillet over medium heat, sauté the meats, onion, and garlic until meat is no longer pink and onions are translucent. Drain in a colander. Return to pan and mix with salt and pepper.

Separate filo dough into 3 piles (about 9 sheets each) and keep covered.

Heat oven to 375 degrees F. Lightly coat a 13- x 9-inch pan with cooking spray. Lay down 3 sheets of filo dough and lightly brush with oil. Repeat two more times until you've used one pile of filo. Spread half the meat mixture on. Then lay down 3 sheets of filo dough from the second pile and lightly brush with oil. Repeat two more times until you've used the second pile of filo. Spread with remaining meat mixture. Then, using the last pile of filo dough, lay down 3 sheets at a time, brushing lightly with oil, until the pile is finished.

Tuck any ends down the sides of the pan and, using a sawing motion and a serrated knife, cut the burek to the bottom into 12 slices.

In a medium bowl, mix together the eggs and oil. Add sparkling water and mix slightly. Pour over the burek and let sit 2 minutes. Bake 45 minutes to 1 hour or until golden brown.

> You can find filo (phyllo) dough in the freezer section in Whole Foods and some other stores; keep in mind that phyllo dough must be out of fridge for couple of hours before use, otherwise it will be sticky and difficult to handle.

Burek with Cheese. *Photo by Nelabooks.*

Burek with Cheese
(Burek sa Sirom)

MAKES 6 PIES

Ingredients

1 pound feta cheese, crumbled
8 ounces cream cheese, softened
2 large eggs, beaten
4 tablespoons chopped fresh parsley
2 tablespoons chopped fresh dill
1 pound filo dough, thawed
    (such as Athens 14" x 18" sheets)
8 tablespoons (1 stick) butter, melted
½ cup good-quality olive oil

Directions

In a large bowl, mix together cheeses until light and fluffy. Add eggs and herbs, mixing well.

Stack 12 sheets of filo dough. Cut filo dough sheets in quarters. You should now have 48 sheets measuring approximately 7" x 9". Cover with damp towel or plastic wrap.

Heat oven to 375 degrees F. Mix together melted butter and olive oil. Using a pastry brush, butter six (8-inch) round shallow pans or two 9" x 13" baking pans (two to a pan).

To Assemble

In first pan, place 2 sheets of filo dough and brush with butter mixture. Repeat with 2 more sheets and butter. Spread one-sixth of the cheese mixture on top and spread to the edges. Layer on 2 sheets of filo dough and brush with butter mixture. Repeat with 2 more sheets. Tuck edges of filo down sides of pan to create a rounded edge. Brush generously with butter mixture.

Repeat assembly layering directions, alternating filo and cheese for 5 remaining pies. Each pie will use 4 sheets of filo on the bottom and 4 sheets on the top for a total of 8 sheets each.

Bake 20-30 minutes or until golden brown.

Christmas Bread (Cesnica). Photo by Ivana Lalicki, Dolce Fooda.

Christmas Bread
(Cesnica)

SERVES 4-6

Ingredients

2 cups milk, warmed to 105 degrees F.
4 teaspoons active dry yeast
4 tablespoons sugar
4 large egg yolks (reserve the whites)
4 tablespoons (1 stick) softened butter
½ teaspoon salt

Sculpting Dough:
1 cup all-purpose flour
1 large egg yolk
Milk, as needed

Directions

In the bowl of a stand mixer or other large bowl, combine warm milk and yeast until dissolved. Add sugar and let stand 10 minutes. Add remaining ingredients and mix thoroughly. Knead 7 to 10 minutes by machine or 15 minutes by hand until a smooth, stiff dough forms and pulls away from the sides of the bowl and your fingers.

Place dough in a bowl that has been lightly coated with cooking spray, turning once to coat both sides. Cover and let rise until doubled. If, when the dough is touched lightly in the center, it springs back, it needs to rise more.

Lightly coat a deep round 9-inch baking pan or the ceramic liner from a small slow cooker with cooking spray. Punch down dough and knead a few minutes to release any air bubbles. Cover and let rise until doubled.

Meanwhile, make the sculpting dough (a non-rising dough that will retain its shape when baked) for the decorations. In a small bowl, mix flour, yolk, and enough milk to make a pliable dough. Pinch off pieces and roll by hand to create the decorations.

Heat the oven to 400 degrees F. When the bread has risen, dip the decorations in the reserved egg whites and "glue" them on. Typically, the bread is divided into quadrants with a braided rope or flat piece of dough in the shape of a cross. Religious symbols, or shapes denoting the occupation or hobby of members of the household, are placed in the four quadrants. A braided rope or flat ribbon of dough around the circumference of the bread is the final touch.

Brush the entire top of the bread lightly, sculptures and all, with egg white. Bake at 400 degrees F. for 10 minutes; then cover loosely with a foil tent and reduce the heat to 350 degrees F. and bake 50 to 60 minutes or until an instant-read thermometer registers 190 degrees. Cool in the pan for 10 minutes; then turn out onto a wire rack to cool completely.

The bread takes a place of honor on the Christmas table along with sprouted wheat that was planted on St. Nicholas Day, walnuts, dried fruit, fresh fruit, and a lighted candle.

Cevapi. *Photo by Tanja.*

Cevapi

SERVES 4-6

Ingredients

1½ pounds pork
1 pound beef
½ pound turkey
1 egg white
4 garlic cloves, minced
1 teaspoon salt
1 teaspoon baking soda
2 teaspoons pepper (black and/or cayenne) to taste
½ teaspoon paprika
1 onion, finely chopped

Directions

In a large bowl, combine the ground pork, ground beef, ground turkey, and egg white. Add the garlic, salt, baking soda, black pepper, cayenne pepper, and paprika. Mix well using your hands.

Form into finger-length sausages about ¾ inch thick. Arrange on a plate.

Cover with plastic wrap or wax paper and refrigerate for one hour to one day, to let the flavors settle and the mixture become firm.

Preheat the grill, medium-low heat. Lightly oil the grilling surface.

Grill cevapi until cooked through, turning as needed. The grilling usually takes about 30 minutes.

Chicken Paprikash with Peas. *Photo by Nelabooks.*

We used Quorn brand vegetarian chicken for the photo.

Chicken Paprikash (Peas Optional)
(Grasak)

SERVES 4-6

Ingredients

2 small onions, chopped
1 tablespoon butter or oil
Water
4 pounds chicken
½ teaspoon garlic powder

1 can peas (optional)
2 stalks celery (optional)
1 teaspoon salt
¼ teaspoon black pepper
1 tablespoon paprika
1 cup sour cream

Dumplings
2 cups all-purpose flour
½ teaspoon salt
¼ teaspoon black pepper
1 large egg, beaten
About ¼ cup water
1 teaspoon paprika

Directions

In a stock pot or Dutch oven, sauté onions over low heat in butter until tender.

Add water until pot is ⅓ full. Add chicken, garlic powder, salt, pepper, and paprika. (If you choose to add peas or celery to the recipe, these can be added along with the chicken.) Make sure water is covering the chicken; if not, add more until it just covers. Bring to a boil and then simmer for 90 minutes, covered, stirring occasionally.

Dumplings

In the meantime, make the dumplings. Mix the flour, salt, and pepper in a medium bowl until combined. Make a well in the center and drop in the egg and about ¼ cup water. Stir and add more water by the tablespoon until you have a sticky dough that just leaves the side of the bowl.

In a separate large pot, boil water. Drop dumpling mixture by the teaspoon into the boiling water. (I use a regular teaspoon from my flatware, not a measuring spoon.) If dumpling mix is too sticky to drop from spoon, then dip the spoon into the boiling water, and the dumpling should slide right off.

When dumplings start floating on top (in about one or two minutes), remove them with a slotted spoon or drain them. You may have to reduce the heat to see when they are floating.

About 30 minutes before chicken should be done, add the dumplings to the pot with the chicken. Add the paprika.

After 30 minutes, you should have a delicious dish: the chicken should be tender enough that it is falling off the bone and the dumplings should have made a thicker sauce out of the liquid the chicken was cooking in. Before serving, add sour cream.

Lentil Soup. *Photo by Ivana Lalicki, Dolce Fooda.*

Lentil Soup

SERVES 4-6

Ingredients

- 1 pound French green lentils (such as du Puy)
- ¼ cup olive oil, plus extra for serving
- 4 cups diced yellow onions (3 large)
- 4 cups chopped leeks, white and light green parts only (2 leeks)
- 1 tablespoon minced garlic (2 large cloves)
- 1 tablespoon kosher salt
- 1½ teaspoons freshly ground black pepper
- 1 tablespoon minced fresh thyme leaves
- 1 teaspoon ground cumin
- 3 cups medium diced celery (8 stalks)
- 3 cups medium diced carrots (4 to 6 carrots)
- 1 small can chicken stock
- ¼ cup tomato paste
- 1 pound kielbasa, cut in ½ lengthwise and sliced ⅓-inch thick
- 2 tablespoons dry red wine or red wine vinegar
- Olive oil, for garnish
- Grated Parmesan, for garnish

Directions

In a large bowl, cover the lentils with boiling water and allow to sit for 15 minutes. Drain.

In a large stockpot, heat the olive oil and sauté the onions, leeks, garlic, salt, pepper, thyme, and cumin for 20 minutes over medium heat or until the vegetables are translucent and tender. Add the celery and carrots and sauté for an additional 10 minutes. Add the chicken stock, tomato paste, and drained lentils; cover, and bring to a boil. Reduce the heat and simmer uncovered for 1 hour, or until the lentils are cooked through and tender. Check the seasonings. Add the kielbasa and red wine and simmer for about 30 minutes, until the kielbasa is hot. Serve drizzled with olive oil and sprinkled with grated Parmesan.

Dill Sauce
(Beli Sos)

SERVES 4-6

Ingredients

2 tablespoon oil
2 cloves garlic
2 tablespoon flour
Bunch dill, chopped
1 teaspoon salt
1 cup milk

Directions

In a sauce pan over low heat, combine oil, garlic, and flour; add dill and mix it all together with salt. Keep adding milk slowly until you get a nice bubbling sauce mixture in about two to four minutes.

Dill Sauce. Photo by Nelabooks.

Djuvec

SERVES 4-6

Ingredients

1 tablespoon olive oil
1 onion, chopped
1½ pounds pork chops
2 tomatoes, diced
2 peppers, sliced
1 cup rice
2-3 cups water

Directions

Heat olive oil over low heat in pan; add onion and pork chops until tender and cooked, roughly about 25 to 35 minutes.

Take onions and chops from the pan and put into a casserole dish. On top of that, add diced tomatoes and sliced peppers. Cover it with rice; then add water (2-3 cups) and put it in oven for 30 minutes at 400 degrees F.

Djuvec. Photo by Nelabooks.

Cheese Danish
(Gibanica)

SERVES 4-6

Ingredients

4 eggs, beaten
1½ ounces ricotta cheese
½ cup ounces cottage cheese
¼ cup cream
1 teaspoon salt
¼ cup olive oil
1 cup sparkling water
1 package filo dough

Directions

Combine eggs, ricotta cheese, cottage cheese, cream, salt, olive oil, and sparkling water. In a greased 9-inch baking pan, layer two sheets of filo, then cover with egg mixture. Repeat for as many layers as you choose, ending with filo on top. Bake at 300 degrees F. for 40 minutes.

Cheese Danish (Gibanica). *Photo by Tanja.*

Koh

SERVES 4-6

Ingredients

6 eggs, room temperature, separated
10 tablespoons sugar, divided
6 tablespoons flour
12 tablespoons Cream of Wheat
Butter to grease pan
1 quart hot milk
1 tablespoon vanilla extract
Berry preserves (optional)

Directions

Preheat oven to 400 degrees F. In a bowl, mix flour and Cream of Wheat. In a small bowl, whisk egg whites with hand mixer until firm. In a large, separate bowl, mix egg yolks with 6 tablespoons of sugar, one spoon at a time. When creamy, slowly add flour mixture. Use a spatula to fold egg whites into the flour and egg yolk mixture. Pour the batter into a greased 9-inch baking dish, or into 4-6 ramekins. Bake for 15 minutes. While cake is baking, heat milk, mixing in vanilla and 4 remaining tablespoons of sugar. Pour milk mixture over cake when it is done. Cool on a rack, then chill in a refrigerator for at least 2 hours. (Serve with berry preserves, if you like.)

Koh. Photo by Ivana Lalicki, Dolce Fooda.

Kommisbrot. *Photo by Ivana Lalicki, Dolce Fooda.*

Kommisbrot

MAKES 1 LOAF

Ingredients

5 eggs, separated
1 cup sugar
2 tablespoons lemon juice
1 teaspoon lemon rind
1 cup flour, sifted with 1 teaspoon baking powder
3 tablespoons water
1 cup raisins, plumped
1⅓ cup chopped walnuts

Directions

Beat egg yolks with sugar for 10 minutes. Add lemon juice and lemon rind to egg yolk mixture. Add flour, baking powder, and water, and stir well. Add raisins and walnuts to batter. Fold in firm beaten egg whites. Pour into ungreased loaf pan. Bake at 325 degrees F. for 1 hour.

Kommisbrot. Photo by Ivana Lalicki, Dolce Fooda.

Potato Salad. *Photo by Ivana Lalicki, Dolce Fooda.*

Potato Salad
(Krompir Salata)

SERVES 4-6

Ingredients

8 slices smoked bacon
2 pounds (about 7-10 potatoes) boiled potatoes with skin
6 scallions, sliced
1 sprig of fresh rosemary, chopped
2 sprigs of fresh thyme, chopped
4 sprigs of parsley, chopped
4 tablespoons vegetable oil
2 tablespoons apple cider vinegar
Salt and fresh black pepper

Directions

Preheat the oven to 375 degrees F. Before you put slices of bacon in the oven, place them on a rack that is put on a baking pan. That way you will get rid of excess fat from the bacon and it will become crispy. It will take around 20 minutes to be done. When the bacon is cool, crumble it.

Peel the skin from the boiled potatoes and slice them.

Slice the scallions and chop the herbs.

Make the dressing by mixing the oil, vinegar, salt, fresh black pepper, and herbs.

Mix everything together, except bacon; then add crumbled bacon on the top.

Potato Salad. *Photo by Ivana Lalicki, Dolce Fooda.*

Chicken Paprikash. *Photo by Ivana Lalicki, Dolce Fooda.*

Chicken Paprikash

SERVES 4-6

Ingredients

2 tablespoons olive oil
1 (2- to 3-pound) whole chicken, cut into pieces
Salt and pepper to taste
1 cup onion, chopped
1 tablespoon paprika
½ cup wine
¼ cup chicken broth
½ cup sour cream

Directions

In a 12-inch skillet, heat olive oil over medium heat and brown chicken on all sides for about 30 minutes. Season chicken with salt and pepper. Remove chicken and set aside.

Add onion to skillet. Cook just until tender, but not brown. Stir in paprika. Return chicken to skillet, turning to coat with paprika/onion mixture. Add wine and broth. Bring to a boil; reduce heat, cover, and simmer for 40 minutes or until chicken is fully cooked and tender. Remove chicken and keep warm.

Boil skillet drippings until reduced to ½ cup liquid, about 3 minutes. Stir in sour cream.

Cauliflower Soup

SERVES 4-6

Ingredients

2 cups water
½ cauliflower, cut into small pieces
1 egg
Salt and pepper to taste
Parsley, for garnish

Directions

Bring two cups of water to a boil. Put in the cauliflower and cook together for about 30 minutes, until tender. Whisk one egg and pour into pot stirring slowly until egg becomes cooked. Add salt and pepper to taste. Garnish with parsley, if desired.

Cauliflower Soup.

Rice and Onions
(Luk I Pirinadz)

SERVES 4-6

Ingredients

2 tablespoons olive oil
1 cup onions, chopped
1 cup rice
2 cups water
Salt and pepper to taste
Parsley, for garnish

Directions

In pan with olive oil, sauté onions over medium heat. Add rice. Keep adding water as rice absorbs. Cook for 10 minutes; then cover and let sit.

Add salt and pepper to taste. Garnish with chopped parsley, if desired.

Rice and Onions. *Photo by Nelabooks.*

Potato Pita
(Pita sa Krompirom)

SERVES 4-6

Ingredients

¼ cup olive oil
1 cup potatoes (2-3, depending on the size of the potato)
1 cup onion, chopped
Salt and pepper to taste
1 pound filo dough

Directions

In a sauce pan with olive oil, sauté potatoes with onions and salt and pepper. In a medium-sized pan, layer the filo dough—one layer filo dough and one layer of potatoes—and fold in two. Bake in oven at 350 degrees F. until golden brown (approximately 30 minutes).

Potato Pita. *Photo by Tanja.*

Mushroom Filo Pie
(Pita sa Pecurkama)

MAKES 4 BIG ROLLS

Ingredients

1 package filo dough
23 ounces button mushrooms (almost 3 cups), sliced
1 large onion, chopped
4 eggs
1 cup sour cream
½ cup canola oil, plus 1 teaspoon
1 teaspoon baking powder
Salt and pepper to taste

Directions

Spray baking sheet with oil. Preheat oven to 475 degrees F. Make two fillings. First filling: heat 1 tablespoon oil in pan over high heat. Add mushrooms and onions. Saute for about six minutes, adding salt and pepper, to taste. Second filling: Beat eggs in bowl, then mix in sour cream, oil and baking powder. On counter, layer five sheets of filo with sour cream filling between layers. Top with vegetables. Quickly roll up filo lengthwise. Repeat to make 3 more rolls. Place 4 rolls on baking sheet, then cut into squares. Bake 15 minutes, then reduce heat to 400 degrees F and bake 15 more minutes until golden.

Mushroom Filo Pie. Photo by Ivana Lalicki, Dolce Fooda.

Cabbage with Sausage and Bacon

SERVES 4-6

Ingredients

2 pounds cabbage, chopped
6 potatoes (medium size)
1 onion
3 sausages
3 slices dry bacon
1 beer, 12 ounces
Salt and pepper
¼ cup egg pastina or penne pasta

Directions

Chop cabbage, potatoes, onion and meats. Put in saucepan with beer, pasta (uncooked), and salt and pepper. Cook on low heat for 30-45 minutes.

Cabbage with Sausage and Bacon. Photo by Ivana Lalicki, Dolce Fooda.

Tomato Sauce

SERVES 4-6

Ingredients

1 tablespoon olive oil
1 tablespoon flour
1 can tomato paste
Salt and pepper to taste

Directions

In a saucepan over medium heat, place a tablespoon olive oil and a tablespoon flour. Mix well and add tomato paste. Mix until smooth and lumps disappear. Cook for about 10 minutes. Salt and pepper to taste.

Tomato Sauce. Photo by Nelabooks.

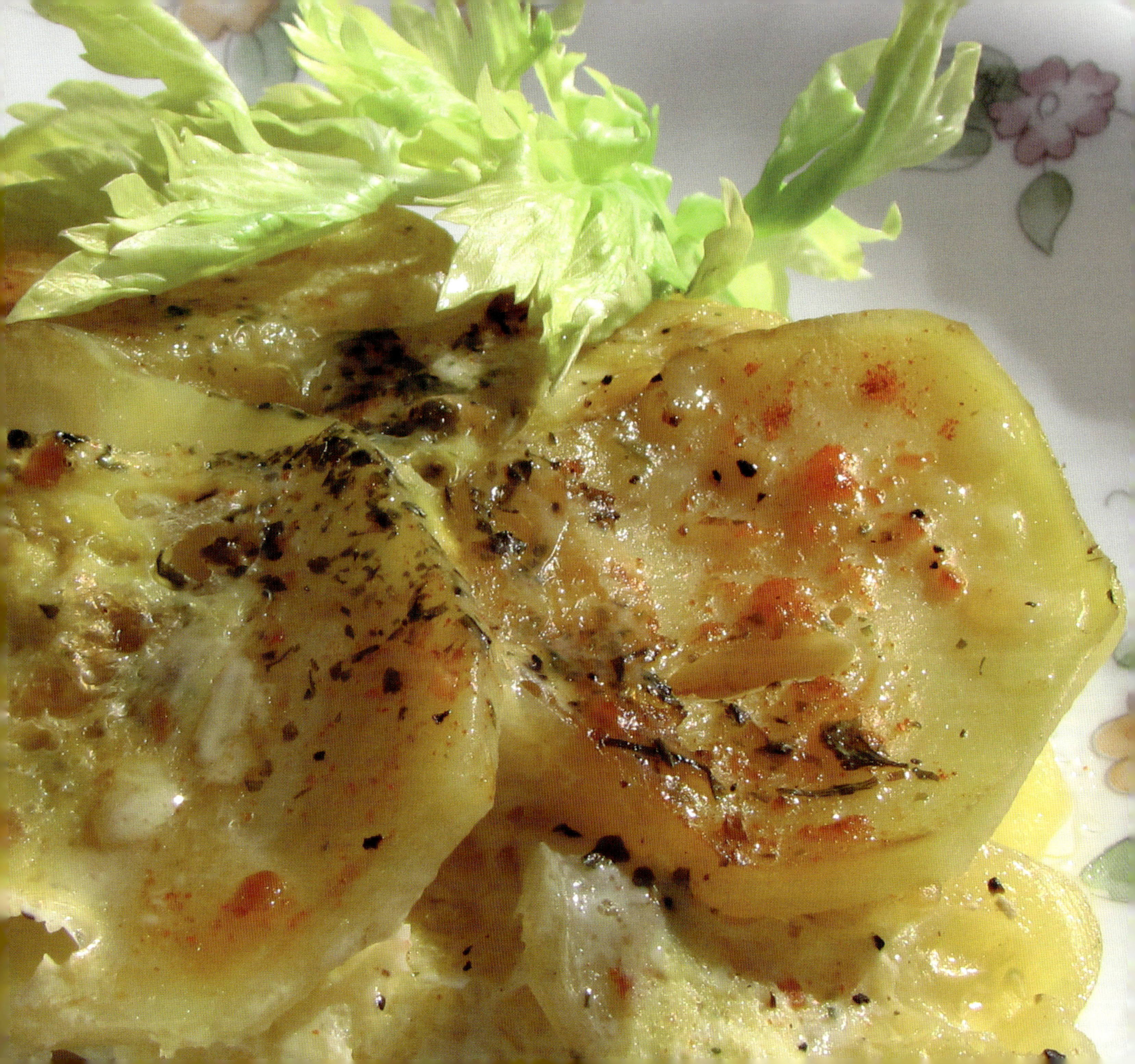

Potato Casserole

SERVES 4-6

Ingredients

5-6 potatoes, peeled and sliced
2 eggs
1 small onion, chopped
Salt and pepper to taste
5 leaves parsley, chopped

Directions

In a casserole dish, place peeled and sliced potatoes. Layer the potatoes on the bottom of dish. In a separate dish mix the two eggs with a fork. After you make a layer of potatoes, pour the eggs and chopped onions over them. Salt and pepper each layer as you go along. Repeat. You should have several layers. Save enough eggs to pour on the top layer. On the top layer add salt, pepper, and parsley. Bake at 375 degrees for about 45 minutes, until potatoes are cooked through. Test it with a fork; if it goes in smooth and doesn't break the potato, the casserole is done.

Baked Beans (Prebranac). *Photo by Tanja.*

Baked Beans
(Prebranac)

SERVES 4-6

Ingredients

1 pound of favorite beans (i.e., black, kidney, soybean)
1 cup olive oil, divided
5 onions, chopped
3 garlic cloves, chopped
1 can tomato sauce with bits of tomato
2 teaspoons paprika
Salt and pepper to taste
1 tablespoon fresh dill, chopped
1½ cups water

Directions

Place beans in 4 quarts water. Bring to boil. Add salt, ¼ cup olive oil and 1 tablespoon of fresh dill. Simmer until beans are tender. Drain, rinse in cold water to stop the cooking process and set aside.

Heat oven to 350 degrees F. In a large covered pot, heat ¾ cup of olive oil and sauté onions until translucent. Add garlic and sauté for 5 to 10 minutes. Add tomato sauce, paprika, salt, and pepper to taste, dill to taste, and water. Mix in the beans, cover, and bake 45 minutes.

Baked Beans (Prebranac). *Photo by Tanja.*

Stuffed Peppers. *Photo by Ivana Lalicki, Dolce Fooda.*

Stuffed Peppers
(Punjene Paprike)

SERVES 4-6

Ingredients

½ cup uncooked long grain white rice
1 cup water
1 pound ground pork or beef (or both)
6 green bell peppers
2 (8-ounce) cans tomato sauce
¼ teaspoon garlic powder
¼ teaspoon onion powder
Salt and pepper to taste
1 teaspoon Italian seasoning

Directions

Preheat oven to 350 degrees F.

Place the rice and water in a saucepan, and bring to a boil. Reduce heat, cover, and cook 20 minutes. In a skillet, over medium heat, cook the meat until evenly browned.

Remove and discard the tops, seeds, and membranes of the bell peppers. Arrange peppers in a baking dish with the hollowed sides facing upward. (Slice the bottoms of the peppers if necessary so that they will stand upright.)

In a bowl, mix the browned meat, cooked rice, 1 can tomato sauce, garlic powder, onion powder, salt, and pepper. Spoon an equal amount of the mixture into each hollowed pepper. Mix the remaining tomato sauce and Italian seasoning in a bowl, and pour over the stuffed peppers.

Bake 1 hour, basting with sauce every 15 minutes, until the peppers are tender.

Ribs on Chef. *Photo by Tanja.*

Ribs on Chef

SERVES 4-6

Ingredients

2 pounds smoked pork ribs
½ cup olive oil
3 ounces red wine
2 tablespoons honey

Directions

Sauté ribs in oil for about 15 minutes. Add wine and a bit of water. When water evaporates, transfer to baking pan and bake at 350 degrees F. for 30 minutes. Halfway through, pour honey over ribs.

Ribs on Chef. *Photo by Tanja.*

Sataras. *Photo by Ivana Lalicki, Dolce Fooda.*

Sataras

SERVES 4-6

Ingredients

3-4 onions
Several tablespoons olive oil
1 tablespoon sugar
8 big red peppers
Paprika to taste and for desired color

1 fresh tomato
1 cup of rice
Salt and pepper to taste
Parsley leaves

Directions

Slice onions and simmer in several tablespoons of olive oil. Add one tablespoon sugar. Slice peppers and add to onions with paprika and some salt. Stew them until they become soft.

Boil some water and pour it over the tomato. Peel and slice it. Place tomato in the stew and continue to stew it until the juice evaporates. Add rice into stew and cook until tender.

Before serving add parsley leaves, salt, and pepper.

Sweet Cabbage with Beef and/or Pork. *Photo by Tanja.*

*You can choose to use nice vegetarian "meats" or beans!

Sweet Cabbage with Beef and/or Pork

SERVES 4-6

Ingredients

3 onions, chopped
About 1 pound beef or pork
⅓ cup olive oil
1 large carrot, sliced
2 pounds fresh cabbage, chopped (1 large head)
1 tablespoon flour

1 teaspoon cayenne pepper
1 pepper, sliced
2 tomatoes
1 cup water
Salt and pepper (peppercorns) to taste

Directions

Cut into pieces and lightly brown onions and beef/pork in ⅓ cup of oil. When the meat is tender, add carrots that have been cut into thin slices, and chopped cabbage. Ten minutes later, add a tablespoon of flour, cayenne pepper, sliced peppers, and tomatoes. Pour water over entire mixture and add salt and pepper to taste. Cover and cook over low heat for about 30 minutes.

Roasted Peppers with Cheese. *Photo by Ivana Lalicki, Dolce Fooda.*

Roasted Peppers with Cheese
(Pecene Paprike)

SERVES 4-6

Ingredients

- 4 large red or yellow bell peppers, preferably Holland
- 2 tablespoons good olive oil
- 1 tablespoon balsamic vinegar
- 2 cloves garlic, minced
- 2 teaspoon kosher salt
- 1 teaspoon freshly ground black pepper
- 2 tablespoons drained capers
- 1 tablespoon ricotta cheese
- 2 tablespoons mozzarella cheese

Directions

Preheat the oven to 475 degrees F.

Place the whole peppers on a sheet pan and place in the oven for 30 to 40 minutes, until the skins are completely wrinkled and the peppers are charred, turning them twice during roasting. Remove the pan from the oven and immediately cover it tightly with aluminum foil. Set aside for 30 minutes, or until the peppers are cool enough to handle.

Meanwhile, combine the olive oil, balsamic vinegar, garlic, salt, and pepper in a small bowl. Set aside.

Remove the stem from each pepper and cut them in quarters. Remove the peels and seeds and place the peppers in a bowl along with any juices that have collected. Discard the stems, peels, and seeds. Pour the oil and vinegar mixture over the peppers. Put it back in the oven.

Mix the ricotta with the mozzarella cheeses together and pour on top, once peppers are done. The cheeses should melt.

DESSERTS

Crepes. Photo by Ivana Lalicki, Dolce Fooda.

Honey Wafers. *Photo by Nelabooks*

Honey Wafers

SERVES 4-6

Ingredients

Dough
8½ ounces ground Serbian biscuits (such as plazma)
2 wafers (such as Oblaten, Oblande, Oplatki brands)
2 tablespoons honey
1¼ cups sugar
1 cup walnuts
14 tablespoons butter
¾ cups water

Directions

Mix the ground biscuits, wafers, honey, sugar and walnuts in a bowl. Combine water and butter over low heat. When butter is melted, add biscuit mixture, stirring into a dough. Remove from heat and allow to cool slightly. Divide into three round balls. Roll out first ball on a cookie sheet sprayed with cooking oil. Layer with glaze. Add another layer of dough by rolling out second ball. Add another layer of glaze, then the final rolled-out ball. Top with chocolate topping.

Glaze
7 ounces cooking chocolate
About ⅓ cup powdered sugar
2 tablespoons honey
1 cup of finally chopped walnuts
5 tablespoons (a little over ½ stick) butter
1 egg

Mix first 5 ingredients in a sauce pan over low heat. Add egg and mix in.

Topping
1 cup chocolate
½ cup heavy cream

Mix ingredients in a sauce pan over low heat until a smooth ganache forms. Pour over pastry when cool.

Baklava. Photo by NelaBooks, courtesy of Balkan Express Restaurant, Philadelphia, PA.

Baklava

Recipe by Ivana Lalicki—Dolce Fooda

SERVES 4-6

Ingredients

1 pound of filo dough
1 cup vegetable oil
2 cups chopped walnuts
2 cups water
2 cups sugar
2 lemons, juice of

Directions

Preheat oven to 350 degrees F. Find appropriate baking pan. If it is small one, you can cut filo sheets and have baklava with more layers. (Mine has dimensions 14- x 10-inch.)

Slightly oil the pan using pastry brush or oil spray.

Unroll filo sheets. While you work cover filo with wet cloth to keep it from drying out. After you set 3 layers of filo dough sheets in the pan, oil and cover it with 1-2 tablespoons of chopped walnuts. Repeat until all sheets are used (the last one should be only oiled).

Cut baklava into small squares or diamond shapes using very sharp knife.

Put it in the oven and bake for 50 minutes.

Cook syrup in the meantime. Heat water until it boils and remove from heat; add sugar, and the juice of lemons. (Add a teaspoon of vanilla extract if you want.) It's done in 20 minutes.

When baklava is done (the top should look crispy and brown), immediately pour hot syrup over it.

After some rest, serve it...with a cup of coffee, of course!

Cupavci. *Photo by Nelabooks.*

Cupavci

SERVES 4-6

Ingredients

2 eggs
¾ cups sugar
7½ cups milk
6 tablespoons olive oil
2¼ cups flour
1 teaspoon baking powder
2 cups finely shredded coconut

Sauce
3½ ounces chocolate
3 tablespoons olive oil and a little butter
6 tablespoons milk
1 teaspoon baking powder

Directions

For the sponge cake
Preheat oven to 350 degrees F. Mix eggs and sugar in a large bowl, then add in milk, oil, flour, and baking powder. Pour into a 9-inch greased pan. Bake for about 30-45 minutes.

When cake is cooled, cut into squares, then dip in warm chocolate sauce and roll in coconut.

Sauce
Melt all the ingredients in small sauce pan over low heat.

Cherry Strudel. *Photo by Tanja.*

Cherry Strudel

SERVES 4-6

Ingredients

Dough
3 cups all-purpose flour
1 large egg, beaten
10 tablespoons butter, melted and divided
½ cup warm water

Filling
¾ cup sugar
1½ pounds Bing cherries, washed, stemmed, and pitted
¾ cup dry breadcrumbs

Topping
Confectioners' sugar

Directions

In a large bowl, combine flour, egg, 8 tablespoons of the melted butter and water. Using a dough hook, mix into a smooth, pliable dough. Wrap with plastic wrap and let it rest for 30 minutes.

Place rack in the middle of the oven and heat to 400 degrees F. In a large bowl, make the filling by combining sugar, cherries, and breadcrumbs. Reserve.

Place a 16- x 24-inch sheet of parchment paper (or tea towel) on a flat surface. Dust it lightly with flour. Roll the dough as thinly as possible until it covers the entire parchment paper (and, in the case of a tea towel, until you can see the design on the cloth through it).

Lightly brush the edges of dough with water. Spread the cherry filling on the dough, leaving a 1-inch unfilled border on all sides.

Using the parchment paper or tea towel to lift the dough, fold the sides in first, then the bottom. Continue rolling away from yourself until you have a nice cylinder.

Transfer to a parchment-lined baking sheet, shape into a horseshoe, and brush with remaining 2 tablespoons of melted butter. Bake at 400 degrees F. for 30-40 minutes or until golden brown. Dust strudel with confectioners' sugar. Serve warm or at room temperature. Garnish with ice cream or whipped cream, if desired.

Bombica

SERVES 4-6

Ingredients

2 eggs, divided into whites and yolks
Almost ½ cup powdered sugar
½ cup cocoa
9 ounces milk chocolate
3-4 tablespoons cream

Directions

Mix the egg whites (for about 10 minutes) into firm peaks and leave to stand aside.
Mix egg yolks with sugar and cocoa, and leave to the side.
Melt chocolate with cream for about 10 to 15 minutes.
Stir until chocolate melts and becomes smooth.
Remove from stove and mix in beaten egg yolks.
Then add the beaten egg whites and mix in.
Roll together into one large ball and many small ones.
Chill in refrigerator for 2 hours and then roll the balls in powdered sugar.

Bombica. *Photo by Nelabooks.*

Chocolate Balls

SERVES 4-6

Ingredients

8 tablespoons (1 stick) butter
½ cup chocolate chips
1 box graham crackers, crumbled (12 crackers)
1 cup of shredded coconut

Directions

Melt butter and chips over low heat.
Add graham cracker crumbs.
Roll into balls.
Leave in fridge for two hours.
Take out of fridge and roll into coconut.

Chocolate Balls. *Photo by Nelabooks.*

Chestnut Cake. *Photo by Nelabooks, courtesy of Balkan Express Restaurant, Philadelphia, PA.*

Chestnut Cake

SERVES 4-6

Ingredients

6 eggs, separated
10 1-ounce squares bittersweet chocolate, chopped
¾ pound whole chestnuts, drained
4 tablespoons unsalted butter
4 tablespoons dark rum
¼ teaspoon salt
½ cup white sugar

Directions

Preheat oven to 350 degrees F. Line the bottom of a greased 9-inch springform pan with parchment paper. Then grease the parchment paper.

Separate the eggs.

Melt chocolate in small pan over low heat

In a food processor, puree the chestnuts with the butter and the rum, scraping down the sides, until the mixture is smooth. Add the melted bittersweet chocolate and blend the mixture until it is combined well. With the mixer running, add the yolks, one at a time, and transfer the mixture to a large bowl.

In a bowl, with an electric mixer beat the whites with the salt until they hold soft peaks, add the sugar, a little at a time, beating, and beat the meringue until it holds stiff peaks.

Whisk about ¼ of the meringue into the chocolate mixture to lighten it, and fold in the remaining meringue gently, but thoroughly. Pour the batter into the prepared pan and smooth the top.

Bake the cake in the middle of a 350 degrees F. oven for 45 to 55 minutes, or until a tester comes out with crumbs adhering to it and the top is cracked. Let the cake cool in the pan on a rack for 5 minutes, remove the side of the pan, and invert the cake onto another rack. Remove the bottom of the pan, invert the torte onto a rack, and let it cool completely.

Glaze
6 1-ounce squares bittersweet chocolate, chopped
½ cup heavy cream
1 tablespoon dark rum
8 marrons glacés (candied chestnuts)

Place the finely chopped chocolate in a small bowl; in a saucepan, bring the cream to a boil, and pour it over the chocolate. Stir the mixture until the chocolate is melted and the glaze is smooth, and stir in the rum. Dip each candied chestnut halfway into the glaze to coat it partially, transfer the chestnuts to a foil-covered tray, and let them set.

Invert the cake onto a rack set on wax paper, pour the glaze over it, smoothing the glaze with a spatula and letting the excess drip down the side; let the cake stand for 2 hours, or until the glaze is set. Transfer the cake carefully to a serving plate and garnish it with the coated chestnuts.

Whipped Cream
1 cup heavy cream
2 tablespoons white sugar
1 tablespoon rum
¾ cup chopped marrons glacés (candied chestnuts)

Make the whipped cream just before serving the cake. In a chilled bowl with chilled beaters, beat heavy cream until it holds soft peaks. Beat in sugar, and rum; beat the mixture until it holds stiff peaks. Fold in the chopped candied chestnuts. Serve the cake with the whipped cream.

Chocolate Rolls. *Photo by Nelabooks.*

Chocolate Rolls

SERVES 4-6

Ingredients

3 tablespoons water
1 cup crystal sugar
7 tablespoons (almost 1 stick) butter
3½ ounces of chocolate
1 sheet large wafers (such as Oblatne, Oblande, Oblatki brands), crumbled
Grated peel of 1 lemon
About 7 tablespoons ground walnuts
About 7 tablespoons ground tea biscuits
1 small bag coconut

Directions

Cook sugar with water over low heat until dissolved. Add butter and chocolate. When melted, mix in wafers, grated lemon peel, ground nuts and ground biscuits. Remove from heat and chill for about 2 hours.

Roll half of dough out into a greased cookie sheet. Layer with half of filling mixture. Roll up into log, then roll log in coconut. Slice into individual servings. Repeat with second half of dough and filling.

White Filling Mixture
3 egg yolks
½ stick butter, softened
3 tablespoons sugar
1 tablespoon vanilla extract

Whisk egg yolks in a bowl, and then mix in butter, sugar, and vanilla extract. Divide in half.

Chocolate Rolls. *Photo by Nelabooks.*

Chocolate Wafers. *Photo by Nelabooks.*

Chocolate Wafers

SERVES 4-6

Ingredients

2½ cups sugar
4 eggs
1 cup of milk
17 tablespoons (a little over 2 sticks) margarine
3½ ounces chocolate

1⅓ cups ground biscuits (12-pack tea biscuits)
1 tablespoon rum
1 packet of vanilla sugar
Almost ½ cup ground walnuts
1 pack wafers (such as Oblaten, Oblande, Oplatki brands)

Directions

In a pot, mix sugar, eggs, and milk; stir and cook until it boils. Add margarine and slowly melt while stirring. Add chocolate and melt. When all is mixed together, add ground biscuits, rum, vanilla sugar, and ground walnuts. Mix all together and assemble on a greased pan by placing a layer of filling and then a layer of wafers until you have used all the mixture.

Crème Puffs. *Photo by Ivana Lalicki, Dolce Fooda.*

Crème Puffs

SERVES 4-6

Ingredients

10½ tablespoons (1¼ sticks) butter
1 cup water
A little over ½ cup bread flour
6 large eggs, separated
Powdered sugar

Cream
6 eggs
12 tablespoons sugar
2 small bags of Jell-O vanilla cook-and-serve pudding (no instant pudding)
4 cups milk

Directions

Preheat the oven to 425 degrees F.

Heat the butter in a 9-inch pan and add water. Bring it to boil and add flour while stirring. Remove it from the heat before it becomes brown.

Beat 6 egg yolks and 6 egg whites separately.

Mix everything together (eggs and dough) with a wooden spoon.

Make about 40 dough balls (1 tablespoon size) using spoon or pastry bag. Place them on a large baking pan, or two smaller ones, making sure to leave some space between balls since they will rise in the oven.

Bake the balls on 425 degree F. for 7 minutes, then reduce temperature to 400 F. and bake for another 13 minutes. Balls are done when they are golden brown and "airy" in the center.

Cut the balls in half when they have cooled down.

Make the cream. Mix eggs with sugar, pudding, and ½ cup of milk. Put the rest of milk (3½ cups) in a pan and bring to a boil; then add the previous mixture stirring constantly. When cream is thick enough, remove it from the heat. Once the puffs have baked, insert the cream. Then put the top back on the puff.

Sprinkle the puffs with the powdered sugar.

Crepes. Photo by Ivana Lalicki, Dolce Fooda.

Crepes

SERVES 4-6

Ingredients

4 eggs
2 cups milk
2 tablespoons sugar
¼ teaspoon salt
2 cups flour
1 teaspoon olive oil

Directions

Whisk 4 eggs; add milk, sugar, salt, and flour, and mix well until batter is formed. Heat oil in a large frying pan. Pour approximately ¼ cup of batter into pan, tilting to evenly coat the bottom. Cook 2 to 5 minutes, flipping once, until golden brown. Repeat with remaining batter.

Add whatever you wish as filling. (Nutella, sugar, jam, preserves, walnuts.)

To make savory crepes, you can add any vegetable just sauté first and add to middle of crepe then wrap and serve.

Peach Pie. *Photo by Tanja.*

Peach Pie

SERVES 4-6

Ingredients

4 eggs
1 cup flour
⅓ cup milk
1 prepared pie crust
10½ ounces peaches (3-4 peaches), peeled and sliced
17½ ounces (1¼ cups) refrigerated, prepared puff pastry

Directions

Mix eggs, flour, and milk over low heat. Remove and let sit until cool. Pour mixture into prepared pie crust (shown here in tart pan). Top with peach slices. Cut the puff pastry dough in long pieces and layer in cross-hatch pattern or lattice on top of peaches (as shown in the photo). Bake at 350 degrees F. for 40 minutes.

Peach Pie. Photo by Tanja.

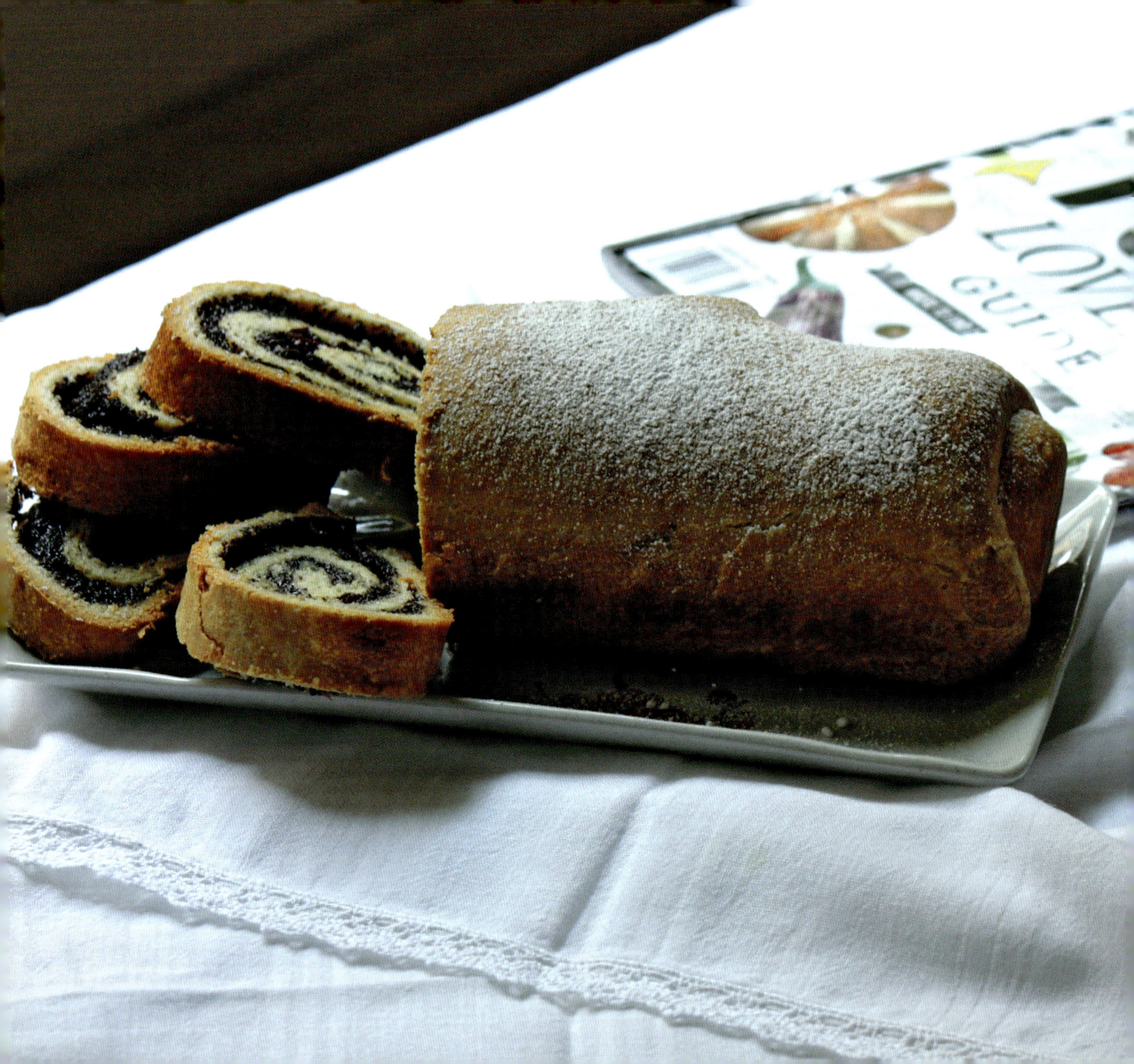

Poppy Seed Strudel

SERVES 4-6

Ingredients

1½ cups sugar
4 egg yolks
1 packet yeast
1½ cup milk

2 pounds flour
Just under ½ cup milk
4 tablespoons olive oil

Directions

Whisk ½ cup of sugar, and egg yolks. Add yeast, 1½ cups warm milk, and flour. Mix by hand until dough begins to break away from the bowl. Divide into 4 equal balls. Each ball should be coated with oil, covered with foil and left to stand until it begins to rise.

Filling
1¼ cups sugar
⅓ cup milk
Almost 1½ cups ground poppy seeds

Bring sugar and milk to a boil. Add poppy seeds, stir vigorously until smooth; then remove from heat.

To Assemble
Roll out dough and spread filling on top. Roll all together and put in oven at 300 degrees F for 30 to 45 minutes.

Slice to serve.

Tulumbe. *Photo by Nelabooks.*

Tulumbe

SERVES 4-6

Ingredients

Syrup
6¼ cups sugar
4 cups water
1 tablespoon vanilla
1 teaspoon lemon juice

Dough
1½ sticks (12 tablespoons) unsalted butter
1½ cups water
½ teaspoon salt
1½ cups all-purpose flour
6 large eggs

Directions (for syrup)

In a large saucepan, bring the syrup ingredients to a boil. Reduce heat and cook down for 10-15 minutes. Let cool completely and then divide into two large bowls.

Directions (for dough and to assemble)

Heat oven to 425 degrees F. In a medium saucepan, melt butter in water. Add salt and flour, and stir until dough forms a mass that cleans the sides of the pan. Beat in the eggs, one at a time, until the batter is smooth.

Line a sheet pan with parchment paper. Fill a pastry bag fitted with a large star tip with dough and pipe 12 (5-inch) lengths onto the prepared pan. Bake about 20 minutes, until the tolumbe puff up and turn golden brown.

Place hot tulumbe into two bowls of syrup, pushing down lightly. Soak overnight and serve cold the next day.

Vanilla Wafers. *Photo by Nelabooks.*

Vanilla Wafers

SERVES 4-6

Ingredients

1 package large wafers (such as Oblaten, Oblande, Oplatki brands)

Filling 1
8 tablespoons (1 stick) butter, softened
Almost ½ cup powdered sugar
A little over ½ cup ground biscuits (tea biscuits) 3½ ounces grated chocolate
1 tablespoon espresso coffee
10 tablespoons milk

Filling 2
8 tablespoons (1 stick) butter, softened
Almost ½ cup powdered sugar
Almost ½ cup flour

Filling 3
8 tablespoons (1 stick) butter, softened
Almost ½ cup powdered sugar
5 hard-boiled eggs (yolks only)

Directions

Make three fillings in three separate bowls: begin each by mixing butter with sugar, then mixing in other listed ingredients. To assemble: Place a wafer on a cookie sheet. Layer the wafer with filling number one. Place wafer on top of filling. Layer wafer with filling number two. Place another wafer followed by filling number three and a final wafer topping. Repeat until all ingredients are sed. Gently press down and refrigerate.

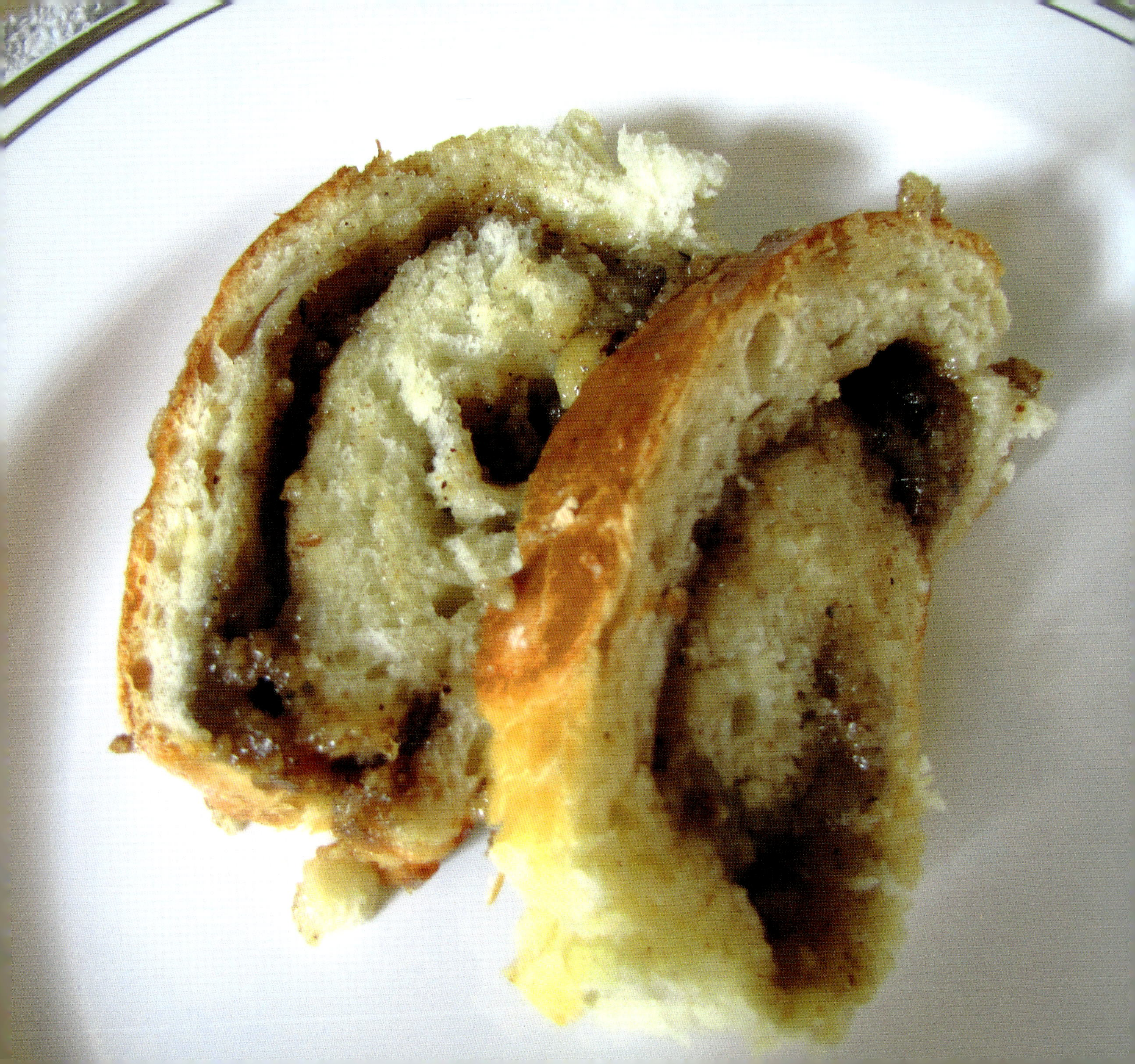

Walnut Strudel

SERVES 4-6

Ingredients

4⅛ cups (a little over 4 sticks) butter, softened
1 egg
4 tablespoons sugar
4 tablespoons milk
1 sachet of vanilla sugar
1 tablespoon baking powder
Orange zest
a little over 1½ cups flour

Directions

Mix all of the ingredients to form dough. Put aside and let rest for 20 minutes.

Filling
Almost ½ cup walnuts, chopped
3 tablespoons milk
3 tablespoons powdered sugar
1 packet of vanilla sugar

In bowl, mix all the ingredients for the filling.

Roll out dough and spread filling on top of dough. Roll the strudel and tuck in, so the filling does not leak while baking. Bake at 350 degrees F. about 30 minutes, until golden brown.

Vanilla Pastry. *Photo by Nelabooks.*

Vanilla Pastry

SERVES 4-6

Ingredients

4 eggs, separated
A little over ½ cup water
1 cup sugar
A little over ½ cup olive oil
1 cup flour
1 tablespoon baking powder

Directions

Dough

In a bowl, whisk the egg yolks, water, sugar, oil, and flour with baking powder.

In a separate bowl, whisk egg whites firmly into peaks and then add to mixture.

Separate dough into three parts and bake each in a greased 9-inch square pan. Bake at 350 degrees for about 45 minutes, then cool.

Filling and Assembly

1¼ cups powdered sugar, plus more for dusting
4⅛ cups (a little over 4 sticks) butter
2½ cups of milk
2 small packages vanilla pudding
4 packets of vanilla sugar

Mix powdered sugar with butter. Put aside in refrigerator.

With the milk, cook vanilla pudding with 4 packets of vanilla sugar.

Cool pudding and then add chilled butter with powdered sugar.

Place first layer of cake on plate. Pour half of the filling on top of cake. Add second layer of cake, and then second layer of filling. Top with cake layer and then dust with more powdered sugar.

Measurements Conversion Charts

Use these tools if you prefer to convert the American standard measurements in this book into metric units. If you prefer to cook by weight, rather than volume, be aware that different ingredients have different weight values, so use a conversion tool (many are readily available online).

Dry Measure Volume Equivalencies

1 teaspoon	0.2 ounces	5 ml
1 tablespoon	0.5 ounces	15 ml
1/4 cup	2 ounces	60 ml
1/2 cup	4 ounces	118 ml
1 cup	8 ounces	225 ml
2 cups (1 pint)	16 ounces	450 ml

Liquid Measure Volume Equivalencies

2 tablespoons	1 fluid ounce	30 ml
1/4 cup	2 fluid ounces	60 ml
1 cup	8 fluid ounces	250 ml
1 pint (2 cups)	16 fluid ounces	500 ml
1 quart (4 cups; 2 pints)	32 fluid ounces	1000 ml = 1 liter
1 gallon (16 cups)	128 fluid ounces	4 liters

Butter Equivalencies

1/8 stick	1 tablespoon	0.5 ounces	15 grams
1 stick	8 tablespoons	4 ounces	113 grams
4 sticks	32 tablespoons	16 ounces	452 grams

Chocolate Equivalencies

1 ounce	1/4 cup grated	40 grams
6 ounces chips	1 cup chips	160 grams

Conclusion

Even though this book contained a handful of some of *my* family's recipes, I hope that you try cooking some of these delicious meals yourself. Maybe you will even be inspired to seek out a Serbian restaurant and sample other delicious cuisine not included here. I especially enjoy the freshness of the food and how a meal can bring a family together. Every year, Serbian families celebrate a family saint day, where friends and family gather for all sorts of delicious dishes. If you are lucky to know a family who celebrates their saint day and you get a chance to go, I would highly recommend it. You will get the opportunity to taste dozens of dishes in one day. And don't even get me started on the cakes!! But, that's another book.

About the Authors

Danijela Kracun was born in Serbia and, at the age of ten, moved to New York. The recipes in this book have been passed down from Danijela's mother and some from her Serbian and Romanian grandmothers.

She and Charles McFadden enjoy family, writing books, meditating, being in nature, walking, hiking, and simple living. They hope their books inspire peace and love.

*If you want peace and love to reign in your life,
you have to be peaceful and loving.*